Poem Said Us

Parker Lee

BookLeaf Publishing

India | USA | UK

Presentation by *BookLeaf Publishing*

Web: www.bookleafpub.com

E-mail: info@bookleafpub.com

ISBN: 9789363300682

First edition 2024

This will be a dual-dedication. First and foremost; I'd like to take a moment to dedicate this to Little Brother, Colton. You were my first friend, and even though I'm supposed to be the older "Big" brother, I find myself learning from and through you always. You keep me humble and down to earth, while holding me extremely accountable. You are the most honorable man that I know and thus the type of man that I strive to be. You truly are My Wealth, and I could not have asked for nor received a better brother than You. Thank you for always being Yourself.

Secondly, I like to take a moment to hold space for and honor my inner child, without whom I'd be unable to be the creative mind that I have grown and evolved into. As the saying goes; if little Me could see me Now.

ACKNOWLEDGEMENT

I am rather grateful to all of the people who have crossed my path along this journey. Some of those I have loved, others I had qualms and quarrels with. All of them have assisted in making me the humble person I am today.

PREFACE

My favorite filmmaker, Tim Burton has always celebrated characters who are dark and misunderstood and strive for deeply personal victories. You will find, dear reader, that the following pages will do the same.

Ode To Coffee

Coffee;
Black,
Brown,
Sugar,
Cream,
Oh How I Love Thee.

Coffee;
Dark,
Bitter,
Bold,
Oh How It Helps To Carry On.

Coffee;
Hot,
Cold,
Iced,
Brewed,
Oh The Various Ways To Consume.

Coffee,
Coffee,
COFF-
EE,
Oh How I Love Thee.

Things Change

Things Change;
Life goes by
Seasons Bloom
It's up to You to Blossom,
Nurture what you Foster.

Hang on, Let go
It's best if you, surrender control
It's journey, it's a ride
Don't you dare to close your eyes, and try not to
hide
Remember, Things Change.

People move on,
Connections wither,
Grow Cold
Color fades
Replay nostalgic memories, in a misty haze.

Thrive

No Matter how Dormant,
Life;
Can and Will
THRIVE-
Again.

Apple Tree Legacy

The apple rarely falls far from the tree.
 I on the other hand fell so hard and fast that I began to roll, generating enough momentum to split in half.
The seeds that spilled out sowed their very own tree.
 For I am, the Master of Manifestation in creating my own destiny and legacy.

Risky Business

Up, Down
Lows, Highs
The Trend
Is Your Friend
The Candlesticks
Do Not Lie
Your Feelings
Irrelevant

Up, Down
Lows, Highs
If You Hang On
It Is A Wild Ride
Bulls
Bears
Condors
Butterflies

Up, Down
Lows, Highs
Their Iron
Meet Your Metal
Delta
Theta
Gamma

ROI

Up, Down
Lows, Highs
Everyone Wants
A Piece
Of The Pie

Levels, Floors, and High Scores
If you're drab and weary
Fret not, nor worry
My withered friend
Things may appear dark and bleak
Your portfolio, rest assured
Will rise to it's peak
By the run of the week
Possibly, the Days End

Wine

Dionysus,
Would assuredly die
Probably first
Plunder about
Then strike you down
If He found out
That you put, Ice
In your Wine

Irony (Ebony and Ivory)

There is no greater
Irony
Than that of
Ebony
And
Ivory

Being (Human)

As to being;
Human,
I believe that we desire to be Loved
Although I believe above All else
We Yearn
To be Understood.

The Scale

Sharp and calculated
Burning and Blinded
By Vengence and Judgement
You will be cut, quick and swift
By the Queen of Swords Herself
Lady Justice.

The Coldest of Shoulders
Is that of the Libra
Who has been born in October
When it comes to the zodiacal
They're rather diabolical.

Hanging in the Balance
Weighing on the mallet,
No one can save You
Not even Lord Thoth,
From a Libra's Wrath
For they, Forget Not.

Return to the Moon

When I part,
with the final beat
of thy heart,
 bestow me in water.

So that I may return,
For I belong
 With the moon,
 to reside evermore.

Tethered

I came for you, I showed up
I even soiled my eyes,
You cannot say that I did not try
Clearly, it was too late,
That was My mistake
Maybe in another life,
We won't give each other so much strife
Once again, we shall be together,
For not only our hearts, but the souls are
tethered.

If Little Me Could See Me Now

I know what it feels like,
To cry myself to sleep
How it is to hurt and to weep
Secrets are meant to be held,
Some things you should not keep
This is what it feels like,
For little me.

Inside
Outside,
Who am I to be
Took a long look,
Into the mirror
Let's find out and see
This is what it feels like,
For little me.

Captain of my soul,
Master of one's sea
Curator of my own domain,
I prefer the waters choppy
Skilled, set, and steady,
For any who dare to stop me.

Carry on, carry on,
Within
Inner me
Energy,
If only
Little Me,
Could see
Me,

Now;

I know that they would be proud
Of how, I've steered the prow
Whilst keeping a clean, cut brow.

A.I. (2025)

A.I., A.I.
Don't be shy
It stands for,
Artificial Intelligence
It makes up for,
Your lack there of it.

A.I., A.I.
Wave
To the old ways,
Goodbye
Digital,
Digital
Overdrive.

Alchemy

Alchemy

Reactive
Equally
Collaborative

If not careful
There may be
A catastrophe

Alchemy

Gold and silver
Bind together
Alkaline, Earth metals

Melting
Melding
Joining in harmony

Alchemy

Venusian

Those ruled by the planet Venus,
Are charming and intellectual
Mastered in the art of seduction,
To others it is merely illusion
Some even grandiose delusion,
Lovers, unless you're mean to us.

For this is what it is to be Venusian:

Mother Aphrodite;
Made us living, breathing Aphrodisiacs
Once our sights are set, on a target,
It's as if you've been hit
By the arrow of Cupid himself,
Thoust finds oneself, loving us back.

For this is what it is to be Venusian:

Picnics in the garden of our medleys,
In a blue swirled daydream
Hypnotized by the words in our melody,
Orchestrating for you the most peaceful
symphony.

Le Grand Orb (La Luna)

Known for a many of years
Known by a many of names,

Centuries, millennia, BC
Why must it always follow me,

Studied
Followed
Worshiped

Greek
Egyptian
Arabic

Many of nights,
We have walked beneath
The light

Many, many mysteries
To whom to we credit,
It's history

When it rises to the peak,
Do You Howl
Are you another one of the sheep

It is inscribed into the stone,
Lest it not have you become
Un-hinged
Luna-tic

Honey (Miel)

Golden,sticky, sweet
Honey
Honey
You cannot be beat.

Honey;
Bees
Suckles
Pie
Mustard
Combs
Bubbles

Is well enough, really left alone
You and all of your intricate structures.

Could you be a whole meal,
de miel?

Little Brother

Little Brother,
We come from the same;
Mother.
Dads, neither of us had
I could ask for no better,
Nor another,
Little Brother.

Solid
Sturdy
Stoic

Little Brother,
Just as I,
You speak, cryptically
Even in verse, ever so poetic.

You go high
While I go low,
Veracity and Valor
Us against any foe
Little Brother, and I.

Tens
Eight

Twos

Four by four,
There are no more,
Sons of David
We Are
Sanders' Born.